Bird Watching Around Ventnor Isle of Wight

Steve Jones

Published by Steve Jones, 2023.

BIRD WATCHING AROUND VENTNOR ISLE OF WIGHT

First edition. June 9, 2023.

Written by Steve Jones.

Table of Contents

Raising funds for wildlife through the Mermaid Atlantic charity row

All author proceeds from the sale of this book will be donated to the Mermaid Atlantic team rowing across the Atlantic to raise funds for the Seahorse Trust, Surfers Against Sewage and Hampshire & Isle of Wight Wildlife Trust.

Three friends, all alike in ambition, are undertaking the ultimate ocean encounter in 2023, The Talisker Whisky Atlantic Challenge. The mission is two-fold, firstly to communicate the detrimental effect of waste items on the ocean and secondly to raise awareness of the power of seagrass and the role it plays in combating the climate crisis.

The 3000-mile row will be an adventure like no other, battling storms, possible marlin strikes and nothing but open water, all while rowing for 2 hours on and 2 hours off for over 35 days.

To discover more about the crew, the row and how you can help the team reach the start line, please visit our website, www.mermaidatlantic.com[1]. Anything you can give in sponsorship or donation to our charities is much appreciated.

Xavier Baker, Paul Berry & Chris Mannion

1. Introduction

The 31st October 1995 was a bad day for me as a bird watcher in the Undercliff of the Isle of Wight. Until dusk, at least...

It was my first year on the island. I'd moved here with my parents and sister in February that year. Seeking a local birding patch, I'd started to cycle from my home in Ventnor to St Catherines Point (St Caths), the southern-most tip of the island and seemingly the obvious place for a 'patch-worker' to concentrate efforts. There are several classes of bird watcher: there are the 'twitchers', ready to travel to any corner of the country to see a rare bird that someone else has found. Then there are the 'patch workers' - they're the bird watchers that concentrate their efforts on finding their own birds on a defined 'local patch'. Then there are the hybrid 'birders'. Birders combined local 'patch work' with bird watching trips and the occasional 'twitch' to see a nice bird someone else has found. I'm a birder, and Ventnor has long been my local patch.

A few other birders worked St Caths in those days, in the 90s, far more I think than now. Sea-watching seemed to take the lions' share of birders attention but I was, and remain, resolutely a 'bush-basher' - searching for grounded landbird migrants in the shrubby vegetation along the coast.

So, back to my bad day that turned good. It was the last day of October and I felt that birding was winding down for the year.

The migrating birds had largely left for Africa. The winds were getting chilly.

But that morning, someone found a Radde's Warbler in Wood Warbler Valley, the wooded area just inland of the open fields at St Caths. Radde's Warbler is one of those autumn birds every serious coastal patch worker on the east coast dreams of finding. They stray to the UK all the way from Southeast Asia, by accident, and in tiny numbers, each autumn.

I got to St Caths early and spent the best part of the day fruitlessly, at times frantically, attempting to get this skulky Asian gem on my life, British, island and patch 'lists'. I'd never before seen a Radde's Warbler, in other words.

All to no avail.

Dejectedly, I emulated the Radde's and skulked off. I cycled home and, two hours before dusk, picked up the dog for a walk.

My house at the time was strategically positioned at a place called Steephill. The garden provided panoramic views over the town and out to sea. But I decided on a walk rather than sitting in the garden.

With binoculars slung over my shoulder - it was getting late in the day and I wasn't intending to look at birds - I took Trigger, my dog, on a walk down the steep steps below the house and onto the Undercliff road. From here we walked the kilometre west to the Ventnor Botanic Gardens.

At that time I was a regular birder in the Botanic Gardens. It felt like a good spot. A bit like Tresco Abbey Gardens, in the Isles of Scilly, but on the central south coast, I thought to myself. Tresco Abbey Gardens, and the Scillies in general, are a classic birding venue, with numerous rare birds found there each year. I'd not found anything notable in the Ventnor Botanic Gardens during those first few months of living locally, so I wasn't really concentrating.

Walking along the path below the café, I approach the Americas Collection. This is simply a collection of trees and shrubs primarily from the Americas.

It also contains three Yew trees.

As Trig rushed ahead to apprehend a leaf, a small group of Greenfinches flitted up from the ground and landed in the Yews.

It was close to dusk. They were presumably feasting on Yew berries pre-roost.

For some reason I decided to get my binoculars that were still slung over my shoulder and scan the bird sat on the topmost twig. I don't know why.

What I saw was a shock.

A big fat head full of stripes! And an orangey tint on the breast and flanks...

Weirdly, I immediately knew what I was looking at.

A first winter male *Rose-breasted Grosbeak*!

For the uninitiated, this is a bird from America that really shouldn't be in southern England. Birders like me dream of discovering such things. In fact, hundreds of us visit Scilly - and Tresco Abbey Gardens - each autumn to find just this sort of rarity.

Panic set in.

The dog clearly recognised that something was not right and ran to my side looking furtive and concerned. She shot me a glance of denial not realising she'd actually flushed a wonderfully rare bird into view. I put her lead on, and we started to run back along the Undercliff road towards home. The sun was setting. It didn't occur to me to hang around to enjoy the bird.

This was long before the advent of mobile phones, and there wasn't a phone box closer than my house.

We jogged the kilometre, largely up hill. I used the land line to phone Dean Swensson, a very experienced Ventnor birder.

I blurted out that I think I've found a Rose-breasted Grosbeak in the Botanic Gardens!

Dean is a super-cautious chap and I was super inexperienced. He asked me to come to his house to check the field guides.

He opened his copy of Lars Jonsson's *Birds of Europe* and there it was - the perfect portrait of my bird!

Sure of the identification, disconcerted by the darkness outside, Dean put the news out. That's what patch workers generally do: if they find something rare on their birding patch, they let fellow local birders know about it.

The following morning dawned fine and sunny. A major Undercliff twitch of seven birders was gathered at dawn, lined up at a safe distance from the row of Yews. Note: had this been on the mainland, and therefore more accessible, there'd have been hundreds of birders gathered at dawn. That's my kind of hell, so I'm glad I live on an island!

Anyway, nothing appeared. The assembled crowd started to shuffle.

Then....a Greenfinch left its roost.

Clearly I was correct in my analysis that these birds had roosted in the Yews.

Then....a bird scrambled into view and worked its way up a Yew branch.

THERE IT IS, two of us whispered.

A Rose-breasted Grosbeak sat in full view.

I was somewhat relieved. The bird, I think about the 16th to be found in the UK at the time, remained around the Botanic Gardens car park for the rest of the day. Very few people visited. But I continued to enjoy my first decent self-found bird in my new local patch.

In the years prior to moving to the island my parents took me to Scilly for a week or two each October, during the second and third week. I was a young teenager getting things like Black Redstart on my life list. I can only think that I'd built a 'search image' of American 'rares' as part of my Scilly birding apprenticeship. That I guess is how I knew it was a Grosbeak. Thanks, Will Wagstaff!

Needless to say, I've tended to stick within Ventnor ever since, rather than travel through excellent habitat on my way to better-watched St Catherines Point.

I've focussed my Isle of Wight birding within the severely under-watched Ventnor Downs, and the Ventnor and St Lawrence portion of the Undercliff, ever since.

This is a superb area year-round.

My hope in writing this short introduction is to induce more islanders and island visitors to work this area and to find nice birds. I also hope one or two of you will move here. Ventnor is home to seven or eight birders, several of whom work this area more-or-less daily.

But it's a big area full of hotspots. We need your help!

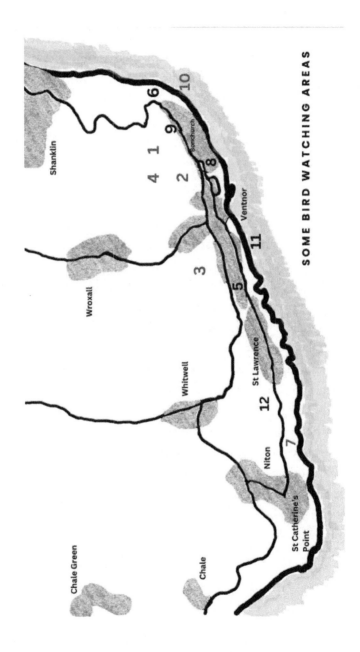

SOME BIRD WATCHING AREAS

6

Chalk downland

1 Ventnor Downs
2 Coombe Bottom
3 Rew Down

Woodland

4 Wroxall Copse
5 Pelham Woods

Landlips

6 The Landslip-Luccombe
7 Binnel Bay-Puckaster Cove

Visible migration

8 Salisbury Gardens
9 Leeson Road car park

Sea watching

10 Monks Bay
11 La Falaise

Inland farmland

12 High Hat area

Towns and Villages

Roads

The sea

2. Overview

Few if any bird watchers looking for an unworked spot to pioneer - find new birding hotspots - will think to look along England's southern coastline. Most of the best spots have clearly been well explored and are well worked by local and visiting birders.

There is one area though. The Isle of Wight. Positioned centrally on the south coast, with better known bird migration hotspots like Portland to the west and Dungeness far to the east, the Isle of Wight really out to attract more attention.

But the relatively expensive car ferries provide real friction, discouraging most mainland birders from casual visits. There are decent foot-passenger services across the Solent and much of the island is criss-crossed by a regular bus service. Even so, few mainland birders visit and genuine twitches to the island rarely take place.

A fair few birders do live on the island. But with a few notable exceptions many of the best areas do not get anywhere near the coverage they deserve.

This short booklet addresses one such part of the island: Ventnor and surrounding areas, forming our south-east facing coastline. It also briefly introduces plans to establish a Bird Observatory.

Ventnor, which here includes the high chalk downland above the town and the adjacent St Lawrence area to the west, has been my main birding patch on and off since 1995.

It's simply superb, especially during migration times when arrivals of birds on the land, and visible bird migration above, can be spectacular.

It's by no means the easiest area to work on the island. It contains an awful lot of bird-hiding cover. Great for hungry birds, not so great for finding them! But the sheer volume of landbird migrants can be a joy. The high downlands that rise to the north above the Undercliff protect it from northerlies and the woodlands, small, scattered streams and wetlands, and warm wooded gardens of the Undercliff provide some intriguing year-round birding opportunities.

For the all-round naturalist

DUE TO THE VARIETY of habitats in a small area, Ventnor and the Undercliff is the perfect spot for the all-round naturalist. And a nature lover based in Ventnor has very easy access to a decent variety of habitats across the island.

Red Squirrels are easy to find in the Undercliff and elsewhere across the island in woodland and well wooded gardens and parks. Dormice are present, mostly in the more open shrubby Undercliff habitats, and Badgers abound.

The invertebrate fauna is impressive but relatively poorly studied; bees and wasps are a prominent group in the friable, south-facing chalk, gault clay and greensand sea cliffs within the Undercliff.

The Glanville Fritillary butterfly is relatively common in its multiple Undercliff colonies.

The species-rich chalk downlands are some of the best in Europe, supporting diverse plant communities and associated butterflies. Adonis Blue and Dark Green Fritillary are present on Ventnor Downs, for example.

The intertidal habitats are rocky for the entire length of the Undercliff shore. These obviously provide excellent rock pooling opportunities.

A few scarce arable wildflowers can be found on the chalk arable above the Undercliff. Field Cow-wheat is perhaps the most notable. This species is currently largely confined to one grassy bank on a Wildlife Trust nature reserve.

I address wildlife generally in a companion book to this guide, called *Wildlife Watching Around Ventnor*. Here, we'll look at the bird life.

Family holidays

IF YOU'RE A BIRD WATCHER and naturalist looking for a family holiday with plenty of things for everyone, the Undercliff is perfect.

There's a wide variety of accommodation for all budgets. Plenty of hotels, guest houses, and self-catering options.

Bank End Farm, St Lawrence, is a prime Undercliff birding site and offers self-catering, caravan and camping options. Closed to the general public, this small area of SSSI farmland is the perfect spot for a birder's family holiday, giving very easy access to a very quiet and beautiful beach at Battery Bay.

Cycling is easy throughout the Undercliff. The main road running the length of the Undercliff now carries very little traffic since one section was taken out by a landslide. That section is now bridged by a cycle track and footpath, giving a wonderful walk and cycle route along the length of the road from Ventnor to St Catherines Point.

If you're based in the Undercliff, all island bird watching spots are within a 45 minute drive and the bus service is good throughout the island.

There are an increasing number of electric vehicle charging spots, including fast-chargers within the central car park in Ventnor town.

Where to eat and drink

HERE ARE SOME SUGGESTED places to eat and drink along the seafront on Ventnor beach.

<u>Besty & Spinky</u>

Right next to the paddling pool, this is the best place for a morning full English breakfast and filter coffee in Ventnor. The paddling pool outside the cafe with numerous tables makes this the spot to take younger kids.

<u>Blakes Tea Hut</u>

Fantastic oat lattes. They use Puro coffee beans and masterfully create the best coffees in town. A percentage of the proceeds from each Puro coffee you buy goes to tropical nature reserve creation via the World Land Trust. Situated on a raised deck on the beach, the tea hut sits opposite the free-to-enter Longshoreman's Museum, which you really should visit. Do please leave a donation for the museum.

Toni's tea room

A favourite spot for afternoon tea, snacks, sandwiches etc., with a nice view across the bay

The Met

Really nice Tapas-style food. The outdoor seating area is lovely on a sunny evening.

Lady Scarlett's

A good range of high quality food with a nice seating area outside overlooking the sea.

Mill Bay pub

Regular live music outside and the best Sunday carvery in town! Very good takeaway meals. You can eat these on the beach, as long as you feed the ever-present Ravens and clear up after!

Golden Sands

Fantastic fish and chips and basket meals and they have lager on tap.

Smoking Lobster

Very good seafood-based meals with a nice outdoor seating area.

Spyglass Inn

Good old pub food, regular live music inside, and the added bonus of a beer garden terrace that overlooks the sea and is perfect for sea watching!

Seapot cafe (Wheelers Bay)

A little way east of Ventnor beach itself, this wonderful little café offers very good food, tea and coffee. Nice sea views for watching Gannets feeding offshore in summer.

There are plenty of pubs, restaurants and cafés within the town centre itself but I rarely visit them so you'll have to find them yourself!

Steephill Cove, just to the west of Ventnor beach, has a little collection of very nice tea rooms and a beautiful small beach for the kids.

Visiting

ONE CAN USE THE CAR ferries or the faster foot ferries that sail from Lymington to Yarmouth (recommended), Southampton to Cowes, or Portsmouth to Ryde. There's also a hovercraft service.

The Lymington car ferry crossing entails far less congestion than the other options and enables one to visit the New Forest when going to and from the island. The short crossing passes through intertidal habitats at Lymington with plenty of waders to sort through if you catch the low tide. You might even be lucky enough to see a White-tailed Sea Eagle fishing for cuttlefish in the Solent!

Moving here

ALTHOUGH THIS SHORT guide is aimed at visitors, the island would certainly benefit from more resident birders intent on pioneering its numerous under-watched areas.

Ventnor is a reasonable-sized town and, combined with Bonchurch, St Lawrence and Niton, presents a range of home options from flats to large villas.

Some parts of Ventnor do suffer from ground movement befitting its status as Europe's largest rotational landslip. But much of the town is essentially stable. Bear this - and thus mortgage and house insurance options - in mind when house-hunting.

If your main interest is grounded landbirds and visible migration, the Undercliff is certainly a good choice for a local patch. Sea-watching can also be interesting, I'm told, but I rarely look out to sea!

If you're more interested in estuary birds, living somewhere in the north of the island, closer to the sheltered Solent coast, is perhaps a better bet. But these areas are very close even if you're based within the Undercliff.

The small Western Yar estuary is easily worked and my favourite area for wading birds. Newtown Estuary is small and attracts decent numbers of waterfowl and waders. The tiny Bembridge Harbour is very easy to work and has the added bonus of small dune systems and the much larger freshwater marshes owned by the RSPB that stretch westward inland.

The three promontories, the Needles, Culver Cliff and St Catherine's Point, each have residential areas within walking distance and various house buying options.

3. What sorts of bird watching?

Dealing with lots of vegetation cover.

Birders visiting the Undercliff may first be struck by the extensive tree and shrub cover. Much of the Undercliff is comprised of secondary Sycamore woodland and well-wooded large gardens. This sort of cover can render birding quite difficult.

The more open farmland strip west of the Botanic Gardens is much easier to work (but isn't worked). Even this farmland strip is backed by a narrow corridor of woodland or well-wooded gardens inland. But this is all wonderful habitat with the capacity to hold birds throughout the day. Migrant birds that arrive early in the morning tend to hang around.

Ventnor Downs are far more open, as is the inner cliff top farmland inland of St Lawrence and around Niton.

Where do you start as a visiting birder?

Hopefully the following site sections in this guide will give some indicators of spots where migrants get concentrated and are easier to count and work through.

Visible migration of landbirds

THIS IS MY FAVOURITE pastime - 'vismiging' - or watching migrating birds as they pass overhead. In autumn especially, I can sit for hours at one of the various bird migration vantage points and just count birds streaming through.

This visible, overhead migration appears to be compressed within the Undercliff, forming a fairly narrow front. At times I'm convinced these birds are following the coast around the island, on a never-ending circuit!

From mid-September one can see flocks of Goldfinches, Linnets and Siskins following the coastline. Meadow Pipits, Tree Pipits, Chaffinches, alba wagtails, Redpolls and Greenfinches pass through in smaller numbers.

Sometimes, movements of Swallows, Sand Martins and House Martins continue throughout the day. Wood Pigeons pass through in sometimes spectacular numbers in autumn, with large clouds high and offshore creating a very odd spectacle. Many hundreds drop into the large Holm Oak woodland on the south face of the downs above the town to feed on acorns in autumn. These are joined by numerous migrant and dispersing Jays. The Jays seem intent on turning our chalk grassland into yet more Holm Oak forest with their industrious acorn planting!

In late September and throughout October, the local populations of Robins, Blackbirds and Song Thrushes swell substantially and individuals of the same three species arrive from further north in colder, continental Europe. Many of these birds are passing through, but some, Robins especially, remain all winter.

Grounded landbirds

SPECIES LIKE NORTHERN Wheatear, Common Redstart, Spotted Flycatcher, Whinchat and various pipits tend to be grounded up on the downs that rise steeply above the Undercliff along its northern, inland edge. These higher peaks are also excellent vantage points to scan for raptors.

I'd suggest working these higher areas during July, August and September, dropping into the Undercliff itself during late September, and, especially, October and November.

Obviously don't rigidly stick to that: the Undercliff can be good earlier in the autumn too, and the downs in late autumn.

It does seem that the first chill of late autumn causes smaller tit-flock-associated birds to vacate the downs and head into the warmer Undercliff.

During both spring and autumn it's worth checking areas of cover around Grove car park, Wheelers Bay, Dudley Road car park, the Winter Gardens, La Falaise, and Ventnor Park, as well as the coastal farmland west of the Botanic Gardens.

Breeding birds

THE FARMLAND ABOVE the Undercliff supports reasonable populations of typical farmland birds such as Yellowhammers and Skylarks. Peregrine Falcons can be seen most days hunting over the town. Ravens are increasingly common breeding species. Buzzards are now very common having recolonised in the late 90s. Little Grebe nests within the Undercliff, as does Long Eared Owl.

Otherwise, the Undercliff supports good populations of all the typical common species of woodland, wooded gardens, towns and the suburbs.

The sea and coast

THE AUTHOR RARELY LOOKS out to sea, so can't give you a well-informed overview of sea bird watching opportunities! However, he did talk to local birder Nick Lever in the pub and here's what he said:

Anything can turn up so putting the time in is what is required. Best chances of seeing some goodies are during south easterlies from March to mid-May or southerlies from August to October. A light breeze is best in the morning and evening. Heat haze and shimmer is a problem in sunny weather but again, visibility is usually best morning and evening.

Winter

NOT THE MOST EXCITING time but there can still be interesting birds. It's the best time to see a grebe and there can be good numbers of Red-throated Diver with up to sixty in a day moving through in flocks of up to ten in what are presumed to be movements between feeding areas. Steve claims that a few loiter to feed inshore off of St Lawrence but this has yet to be confirmed by competent birders [author comment: noted]. The occasional Great Northern Diver flies through. There is often a trickle of auks, Gannet and Kittiwake, and sometimes larger movements, usually in winds between south and west. Gannets will often mill about feeding. Gales in late November 2022 and early January 2023 produced Leach's Petrel.

Spring

THE MOST PRODUCTIVE season, especially if the wind is in the eastern sector, ideally south-easterly. Late February through March is a good time for Brent Goose and dabbling ducks. Scoter passage picks up in April and continues into May. Check flocks of Common Scoter for Velvet Scoter and other ducks. Skua passage picks up in April and continues into May. Great and Arctic Skua are regular and Pomarine is seen on a few days each year (my best flock is six). Most Skuas are fairly far out but a few come close in.

Garganey is regularly picked up offshore during April.

The only waders seen in decent numbers are Whimbrel and Bar-tailed Godwit. Whimbrel have a protracted passage but most of the Bar-tails pass through between 18th and 28th April. The best time for big flocks of godwits (up to 150) is in the evening and most of the flocks are quite far out.

Manx Shearwater are regular and can come close in. The best time for them is in the evening in the last hour before sunset.

Terns are regular but usually in small numbers. Sandwich is most common and 'Commics' are occasionally accompanied by Little Gull. Black-throated Diver is regular in late April and May and can be close in.

The beauty of sea watching [author note: about the only redeeming feature of sea watching] is you can also get birds coming in, off the sea. Hirundines and Swift, Marsh Harrier, Alpine Swift, Cattle Egret and a Hoopoe that was singing in a tree at the end of St Catherine Street were all detected during sea watches.

In murky conditions one recent late autumn, Blackbirds and Song Thrushes could be seen coming in from out to sea, with several exhausted birds taken by Herring Gulls as they approached the shore.

Summer

EVENINGS CAN PRODUCE flights of Manx Shearwaters but some years are better than others. I've seen a flock of 200 Common Scoter flying east in June. There can be good numbers of post breeding Mediterranean Gulls in July/August and it's worth looking out for juvenile Yellow-legged Gull and Balearic Shearwater. [editor note: there is what I assume is a pre-roost gathering spot at Flowers Brook, and I've picked up decent numbers of Mediterranean Gulls there in the past]. The odd Little Egret feeds along the rocky Undercliff shore and can sometimes be picked up flying between favoured areas.

Autumn

SOUTHERLY WINDS ARE ideal but anything from south-east to south-west is good (ideally not gale force). A Fea's Petrel was Nick's best recent bird offshore. September is best for Manx and Balearic Shearwater plus the chance of skuas and terns. October is best for Sooty Shearwater with duck passage carrying on into November. There can be big movements of auks e.g. 1000+ Razorbill on the 22nd September 2022.

Nick's account above I hope illustrates that the stretch of south-east facing coast between St Catherine's Point in the west and Monk's Bay in the east is well worth watching. Nick is I think the most persistent sea-watcher in the Undercliff away from St Catherine's Point.

In terms of spots to watch the sea from around Ventnor, I'd suggest the following:

Monks Bay: east of Ventnor in Bonchurch (my impression is that some sea birds swing in a little closer to this south-east facing tip of coastline). You can park in the Shore Road Pay & Display car park and scan from that elevated position, or walk down to Monks Bay and sit on one of the benches half way up the slope to East Dean.

Wheelers Bay: there's a helpful bench in a fairly sheltered spot just above and west of the cafe. The deck of the cafe here is another option, although this is a bit low relative to sea level.

Salisbury Gardens: an elevated area of public open space with various benches offering shelter depending on wind direction. Also excellent for visible landbird migrants overhead.

Spyglass Inn deck: the beach side beer garden of this pub is a little low but offers the opportunity to enjoy a summer evening pint while scanning for Manx Shearwater! Also does decent pub food and filter coffee...

La Falaise Car Park: Just above and west of the pub, the pay-and-display car park is a good height and you can sit in your vehicle to scan.

There are doubtless further good vantage points further west in St Lawrence but these are yet to be discovered. One likely spot is Woody Head.

The White-tailed Sea Eagles

AS MANY WILL KNOW, the Isle of Wight is providing the launchpad for the reintroduction of White-tailed Sea Eagles to southern England.

Although Sea Eagles are now present year-round on the island, it's not necessarily the easiest place to see them.

I'll provide a brief account of the project here, with some tips for seeing the birds. But I suggest one doesn't make seeing eagles a primary purpose of visiting the island!

At the time of writing (May 2023), juvenile eagles have been released from the island over several summers. As is normal for juvenile eagles, they are wide-ranging and come and go, visiting areas across southern and northern England, Scotland and, on occasion, the near continent.

Some of these eagles are coming of age and have paired up in suitable habitat on the mainland. One pair includes parts of the island within its large home range.

Over time, pairs will hopefully form across the country from this reintroduction. Because the birds range far and wide, the island isn't really a reliable place to see them (although there are several present most days).

Probably the best strategy is to check the Solent coast and estuaries in the north of the island.

The author has only twice seen one of these eagles from within Ventnor, illustrating just how difficult they are to see!

In time, the birds will mature and settle in. More details of where exactly to see them will likely be provided in a future edition of this guide.

Bird watching in winter

I DON'T TEND TO STAY in the UK during our winter so can only provide some broad suggestions.

Essentially, the whole of the Undercliff provides a nicely sheltered enclave within which birds can escape frosts and cold northerlies. Its scattered streams, small pools, the odd reed bed and stands of wet willows no doubt support things yet to be discovered. Wintering Chiffchaffs are usually present at various wet sites and Blackcaps are usually numerous in winter, often sub-singing somewhere close to a garden feeding station. I estimate that about ten Black Redstarts spend each winter within Ventnor.

My impression is that the offshore area at St Lawrence gets regular feeding divers, having seen several a couple of winter's back, but this needs to be investigated.

Personally, if I was a birder forced to remain in the UK over our winter, I'd hide in the Undercliff!

It's worth venturing out of the Undercliff to check the stubble fields on the farmland on top of the inner cliff face. Farmers here deliberately provide spring barley and retain weedy stubble for farmland seed eating birds. Some of this habitat is crossed by public rights-of-way. Without doubt, interesting birds might be found amongst the numerous wintering Yellowhammers if people searched.

4. Bird watching spots around Ventnor

I've attempted to divide Ventnor and the Undercliff into a number of fairly distinct sectors, to serve as a site guide and so readers can orientate themselves and narrow down where to go. You can view YouTube videos of these various spots and a video of maps on the channel linked to at the front of this book.

Below, those sectors are split between the Undercliff itself and the higher downlands and farmland just inland and above.

I rarely leave the Undercliff but will provide a very brief overview of other island spots later in this guide.

4.1 Within the Undercliff

STRETCHING A LITTLE under ten kilometres between St Catherine's Point in the west and Bonchurch in the east, the Undercliff dominates the island's south east coastline. From the south-facing shoreline with low chalk, greensand and gault clay sea cliffs, a low-lying terrace extends by an average of 500m inland to a high greensand and chalk inner cliff. Above this inner cliff face, outside of the Undercliff, are the high chalk downs and mixed farmland.

The high inner cliff protects the Undercliff from chilling northerlies and this, combined with the whole area's south-east facing aspect, explains its warm climate. Snowfall is infrequent within the Undercliff, but regular on the downs just above. The apparently sub-tropical Ventnor Botanic Gardens attest to its year-round mild climate; it's said to rival Tresco Abbey Gardens in terms of warmth if not coverage by birders. Tresco likely receives more coverage during an October morning than our Botanic Gardens sees in a decade! The warmth also explains why Wall Lizards and Glanville Fritillaries thrive around Ventnor and why the area is favoured by late-to-move migrant birds later in the autumn. It probably also explains the dramatic proliferation of Holm Oak throughout the Undercliff. This species will likely come to dominate Undercliff woodlands in the coming decades and one can only hope that its associated Iberian biodiversity arrives too to render it less boring!

I have identified four 'sectors' in the Undercliff as follows:

Ventnor town

VENTNOR TOWN ITSELF offers many opportunities for fairly typical urban building. Its potential is of course elevated somewhat by its coastal position.

Recent birds seen within or from the town include Fea's Petrel, Dark Eyed Junco, Pallid Swift, Alpine Swifts, Red Rumped Swallow, Crag Martin, Bee Eaters, Serins, Wrynecks, Golden Oriole, Hoopoes, Blyth's Reed Warbler, Radde's Warbler, Yellow Browed Warblers and Great Spotted Cuckoo.

The town is hilly, with numerous steep, residential roads, lanes and public paths and steps to walk up and down and some large gardens and sycamore clumps scattered around town drawing in migrants.

At night the lights of the town are obvious from offshore. These lights presumably draw night time migrants in.

The town itself is rather under-watched, and would probably reward additional, concerted coverage.

Below, I identify a few of the best spots in the town. It's worth bearing in mind that some patches of seemingly good cover in the town inexplicably attract very few migrants. A few tens or hundreds of metres away another patch of cover, which to the human eye looks no different to the first, will consistently draw in and hold birds.

Discovering these idiosyncrasies requires at least several years of intense patch stomping. For example, although I first started birding here in 1995, it's only in the last four or five years that I've discovered that Spotted Flycatchers predictably favour certain tree clumps. I really struggled to find any at all within the town before discovering these few favourite spots.

I should stress, though, that, in early Autumn at least, Ventnor Downs around the Radar Station, Coombe Botton etc, are far more productive in terms of numbers of grounded birds than the town itself. You'll likely build far better counts of common migrants up on this higher ground than by flogging the town. The areas of sparser cover within the town mentioned below may be better for finding oddities. You might discover other good spots.

<u>Within the town</u>

With rather less tree cover than elsewhere in the Undercliff, the more fragmented cover in gardens and Sycamore clumps around Ventnor itself can be productive, particularly later in the autumn when migrants seem to vacate the wind swept downs above.

I simply walk the streets of Ventnor throughout the spring and autumn, checking various copses and wilder gardens. Visible migration above can sometimes be rather spectacular, and parties of thrushes, Chaffinches and Goldfinches often settle briefly in tree clumps before moving on. Starlings are not resident anywhere within the Undercliff but pass through in small numbers in spring and autumn.

Ventnor East Cliffs: this area extends from the east side of Ventnor Bay east as far as Wheelers Bay (see below).

The lawns around Salisbury Gardens are an excellent vantage point from which to count visible migrants. On some autumn days, the heavy passage of Swallows continue from just after dawn late into the evening. Pied Wagtails, Meadow Pipits, Goldfinches, Chaffinches, Siskins, Redpolls etc move in good numbers.

The lawns attract a few Wheatears in spring and autumn, and these often feed on the outer breakwater rocks of the harbour below. The scrubby patches at Alexandra Gardens, Devonshire Terrace, and in front of Dudley Road car park are attractive to grounded migrants. The Tamarisks fronting Devonshire Terrace can be very attractive once they leaf-up in mid May, and Phyloscs love them again in the autumn.

The **Bath Road to Alma Road** public path, above the Spyglass Inn in Ventnor Bay, has a small Sycamore clump that small numbers of migrants gravitate to. A Long-tailed Tit flock is a fixture here every autumn and winter, and in autumn draws in Chiffchaffs, Willow Warblers, Goldrests and a few Firecrests. Wintering and breeding Blackcaps are conspicuous here and wintering Black Redstarts favour the small patch of allotments above the Longshoreman's Museum just to the east.

La Falaise: the shrub and Sycamore covered slopes on the inland edge of this car park, on the west side of Ventnor Bay, can be attractive to migrants, though it's very dense. I found that one particular small group of open, diseased Ash trees are very attractive to Spotted Flycatchers in autumn. Later, as the Sycamore leaves are thinned by autumn gales, this area is easier to search. The shoreline below is rocky with soft chalk cliffs well known for their scarcer bees and wasps. Kingfishers and a Little Egret often visits the rocks here in autumn and winter, as do Common Sandpipers and Oystercatchers. A pre-roost gathering of gulls around the disused sewage outflow just west at Flowersbrook attracts a few Mediterranean Gulls in late summer. The car park is a good spot from which to scan the sea.

Grove Car Park: an area of Sycamores around Grove pay and display car park next to St Catherine's churchyard. During late autumn this little area has consistently proved a real migration trap, with good concentrations of Chiffchaffs and Goldcrests, Firecrests and Blackbirds and Song Thrushes in the cemetery and around the car park itself. This area is close to the sea so is bound to pick up good birds (and has at least one Yellow-browed Warbler record and, recently, a single Golden Oriole). More ought to be found if people drop in more often.

Wheelers Bay: One of the better Serin spots in the town (although that might just be down to the small concentration of resident birders here!). The private, weedy gravel car park here attracts groups of feeding Goldfinches and a feeding Serin once. A Great Spotted Cuckoo frequented this area and the coastal cliffs to the east for an extended period one recent spring, feasting on Glanville Fritillary catterpillars.

The small copse and rather sparse cover around the small group of chalets is attractive to migrants and well worth regular visits in spring and autumn. Two Wrynecks have been seen here in recent years (both in different birder's gardens!), and a Melodious Warbler once. The little Tea Room down on the seafront here has a terrace that's good for sea-watching and sells very good food with excellent sea views.

Zig Zag Road: walk up and down this quiet but steep road discretely checking Sycamore clumps and gardens. I've found several autumn Yellow Browed and a trilling spring Wood Warbler here. Migrants will be passing overhead during the right seasons. This is another area favoured by autumn Black Redstarts, feeding on ever-popular Cabbage Palm fruits.

Ventnor Bay: Check rocks west the bay for infrequent, or just unobtrusive, wintering Purple Sandpipers. Ventnor Haven outer arm is probably a good spot for a seawatch, but you'll be at sea level. Wheatears really love the outer rock arm in spring and autumn.

Those Cabbage Palms: the white berries of this species are attractive to numerous species, not just the Black Redstarts mentioned above. They are common throughout the town and every one with berries in autumn and winter should be scanned. We still need Red Eyed Vireo for Ventnor and it'll be feasting on Cabbage Palm fruits!

Ventnor Park

VENTNOR PARK IS ESSENTIALLY a sycamore woodland with more open lawns and flowerbeds just above the sea cliffs on the west side of Ventnor Bay.

It's a popular local park but, thankfully, does not get anywhere near as busy as similar parks on the mainland. It can therefore provide a relaxing and productive spot for birding.

It consists of an east-west running ridge, with tree- and shrub-covered slopes south down to the beach, and parkland with Sycamores on the north slope, down to a small stream. The southern, sea-facing slopes can prove extremely productive during from September - November. Decent parties of Chiffchaffs gather in the sunny, scrubby sycamores; the odd Spotted Flycatcher favours the sun trap along the ridge top later in the day as the last of the sun warms up the slope above Flowersbrook. The cascading stream leading down to Flowers Brook here is a favourite watering hole for Phyloscs, Grey Wagtail, thrushes and who knows what else.

The ridge top east of the outdoor gym is an excellent vantage point for visible migration watches, although views north are somewhat curtailed by the Sycamore woodland. The most notable recent rarity there was a Radde's Warbler in October 2020.

Being essentially woodland, locating birds can obviously be tricky. In spring, it's probably best to listen out for distinctive songs and calls. A single tit flock forms in autumn and works its way back and forth through the park from Flowersbrook to The Terrace on Bath Road, never deviating from that circuit. The scattered Yews near the bandstand are the best spots for Firecrests.

Yellow Browed Warbler appears annually in ones or twos, and probably more with concerted observation.

Although best for woodland birds there are pockets of more open shrubs both at the sea cliff edge and at the top of the ridge line that dominates the south slope of the park down to La Falaise.

The lawns by the stream and around the bandstand are very popular with autumn thrushes.

Red Squirrels are of course common but can be shy. Sit on one of the benches by the band stand and scan the surrounding canopies.

I've long predicted a Red-flanked Bluetail or Olive Backed Pipit within Ventnor Park! Please put the news out when you find one...

Ventnor Botanic Gardens, Steephill Cove and Pelham Woods.

THIS AREA INCLUDES mature parkland and public gardens, a wonderful cove with cafe and a Sycamore-dominated Local Nature Reserve at Pelham Wood.

Ventnor Botanic Gardens can be good for all the common migrants and hosted a fine first-winter Rose-breasted Grosbeak for a couple of days at the end of October/early November 1995. Yellow Browed Warbler and Golden Oriole have appeared more recently but the gardens are only very infrequently visited by resident birders.

Pelham Wood is particular good, being a reliable spot for Firecrests in autumn and winter and producing Yellow-browed and Pallas's Warbler. Check the public path (Paradise Walk) that descends from Whitwell Road, hugging the inner cliff face. This is a real sun trap and birds gravitate to the cliff-face shrubs, Ivy and Sycamores. Connect with a late autumn tit flock and you never know what you'll turn up....

Old Station Road

HIGHER UP, AT THE TOP edge of Ventnor town, sits Old Station Road. An old quarry at the base of Coombe Bottom, forming a south-facing valley, this area is favoured by Phyloscs and crests, often in with the local Long-tailed Tit flock later in the autumn. Although no longer covered with any regularity, this area usually gets Yellow-browed Warbler later in the autumn.

The Sycamores lining the industrial estate quarry are split from a second small copse on the seaward side of Ocean View Road, and birds frequently cross between the two areas. A narrow bank of chalk scrub follows Ocean View Road west to the Old Shute where there's a further Sycamore clump again dissected by Ocean View Road, and tit flocks frequently commute between the Old Shute clump and the Old Station Road.

There's a public footpath encircling the top edge of the industrial estate, giving access to the Sycamore copses and also the excellent Coombe Bottom. This bowl of chalk grassland is simply superb for wildflowers and butterflies and, in spring and autumn, very attractive to migrants.

To me, it feels like a Cornish Valley. Except it gets considerably more common migrants!

The berries on the species-rich shrubby slopes are feasted upon by thrushes as autumn progresses. You can walk up through Coombe Bottom and up onto Ventnor Downs, viewing the shrubby slopes either wide.

Bank End Farm to Old Park, St Lawrence

ONE OF MY FAVOURITE birding spots! The Undercliff is about 500m wide here, and the entire coastal stretch is active, increasingly wildlife-friendly farmland from the Botanic Gardens west to Binnel Bay.

As detailed in the introduction, the various accommodation options at Bank End Farm render this the perfect place to stay for visiting birders. Those staying at the farm have access to the fields and can search its various habitats. Alternatively, the very quiet coastal path here provides good views both inland across the narrow strip of farmland and out to sea.

The 'wader scrape' (a shallow farm pond) at Bank End Farm above Battery Bay usually has a decent muddy zone in spring and autumn to draw in the occasional wader. Birders rarely check although it is in full view of the coastal path. Little Grebe, Moorhen and Mallard nest here, and it's a favourite spot for Wheatears and Whinchats.

The shrubby cliffs at Battery Bay can be excellent for migrants and is a favoured spot for spring Grasshopper Warblers. The island's first Eastern Subalpine Warbler spent a recent April day in the flowering Blackthorn here. Check the small streams, reed beds and wet willow clumps along the coastal path.

All sorts of migrants congregate in these cliff top habitats as one might expect. Walk further west along the coastal path to Woody Head. This is a great vantage point from which to watch visible migration, and a Wryneck spent a day feeding on the cliff top path here in autumn 2013. A few waders visit the rocky coves below, and will roost on larger offshore rocks protruding from the sea at high tide. The weedy cliff faces within the coves attract small parties of Goldfinches and Linnets.

The coastal fields in front of Old Park are much favoured by Wheatears and the patches of shrubs around the pill boxes look very shriky. I'm sure a Rufous-tailed Rock Thrush will appear here at some point.

Looking inland from the coastal path, you'll see a continuous belt of Sycamore woodland and large, well-wooded gardens. Red Squirrels are present, as elsewhere in the Undercliff. Barn and Long Eared Owls nest. Don't be put off by the amount of cover: simply listen out for a roving tit flock, particularly later in the autumn.

An early morning visit in April/May is a must to experience the deafening dawn chorus.

The large villas with spacious gardens look and feel perfect for rare birds! One can just imagine an American thrush hopping around on one of those lawns, or, more realistically, a Wryneck on one of the numerous dry stone walls. The streams that cascade from the inner cliff face and flow towards the sea cliff are a haven for feeding migrants. I'd suggest you simply wander round the quiet lanes of St Lawrence peering discretely into likely spots - migrants can literally be anywhere. But please respect householder privacy.

A perfect morning 'loop' would entail parking at the Botanic Gardens (minimum spend ten pounds), getting onto the coastal path through the gardens and walking west past Orchard and Battery Bay to Woody Head, then striking inland at Woody Bay Cottages. From here you can walk north east up to Woolverton Road and join the Undercliff Drive. Then walk back east to the Botanic Gardens. You can do the same loop if you're staying at Bank End Farm by entering the coastal path via the guest gate from the farm. This route takes in examples of all the main Undercliff habitats.

Bonchurch

I'VE ALWAYS FOUND BONCHURCH something of an enigma. It *looks* like it ought to be superb. But, on the whole, I consistently fail to find much in the way of migrants here. Even autumn tit flocks seem elusive.

That said, Monk's Bay is both an excellent little migrant trap and offshore seabirds seem to swing in closer here as they follow the coast.

Recent quality birds include Crag Martin (briefly over the East Dean Centre), Golden Oriole and the Great Spotted Cuckoo just along the esplanade towards Wheeler's Bay.

A pair of Serins spend a day in the 90s feeding on a landslip behind the Monk's Bay toilet block one March and are no doubt regular.

The two churchyards are wonderful. A Yellow Browed Warbler was present in the old churchyard one recent autumn, while the newer (but still very old!) church yard is very good for thrushes in autumn. Firecrests breed widely in Bonchurch and so can be encountered year-round.

Bonchurch Pond isn't as productive as one might think, but does have its wintering Kingfisher. It's a likely spot for a Night Heron given the marshy area and willows. Conditions there may well have improved recently after the very dense shade was greatly reduced by removal of many Sycamores. It's now far warmer and sunnier than when I made regular visits.

Red Squirrels are present throughout, and Glanville Fritillaries are common along the esplanade.

Undercliff Drive west of Old Park

A FEW YEARS AGO, A land slip destroyed two short sections of carriageway on the hitherto rather busy Undercliff Drive, the main coastal route through the Undercliff from Ventnor to Niton.

Due to on-going instability and a 'do little' policy stance along this stretch of coastline, the decision was taken to close this section of the road to through traffic.

A pedestrian and cycle path was installed across the damaged section of road and, today, this road has become a very tranquil footpath and cycle route with only relatively infrequent cars.

One can still drive along this road either side of the closure.

It's now also a superb, year-round birding trail through coastal woodland, active landslips and well-wooded gardens.

Although rarely visited by birders, this section no-doubt would reward more concerted coverage.

Recent rarities have included the authors' only Undercliff Pallas's Warbler, several Yellow Browed Warbler, Melodious Warbler, Red-footed Falcon and possible Red-throated Pipit.

Binnel Bay to Puckaster Farm

THIS IS A LONG STRETCH of largely inaccessible coastal land slip and shoreline. Although large parts are effectively inaccessible, there are a number of informal paths created by a few local dog walkers. Nobody goes birding in this area. It looks superb. Go and explore!

4.2 The chalk downs above the town

AFTER BEING IMMERSED in the often-dense cover of the Undercliff, the open, windswept downs and farmland above can be a relief. Here, birds more typical of lowland farmland are reasonably common, and migrants rarely encountered within the Undercliff can be sought.

Ventnor Downs, Steephill Down and High Hat are the most straightforward areas to cover. But good spots abound.

Ventnor Downs

LARGELY OWNED BY THE National Trust and entirely within conservation-focused management, the high chalk downlands tower above Ventnor affording it shelter from northerlies.

The higher-altitude habitat is diverse, with the gravel cap supporting acid grassland and chalk heath, complementing the open species-rich chalk grassland, shrublands and sheltered Ash woodlands.

The heather-clad chalk heaths seem to be most attractive to both Lapland Bunting and Snow Bunting. The area of Bracken that fills the Bowl seems to draw in Grasshopper Warblers and Wrynecks.

The Rim - the ridge line that encircles Coombe Bottom along three edges - is especially attractive to chats, flycatchers and Phyloscs. The fence lines marking the Rim edge are used by groups Spotted Flycatchers while the open shrubby chalk heath either side is favoured by Redstarts.

The open sward with scattered gorse and bramble clumps along the north side of the main access road is excellent for

Skylarks and Meadow Pipits in summer and attracts decent numbers of migrant pipits in Autumn.

The scrubby edge directly east of the dew pond can be fantastic for concentrations of warblers, chats and flycatchers. Further east, Nansen Hill is a real sun-trap and, again, much loved by Redstarts and flycatchers.

The close-cropped grassland around the radar station is great for Wheatears whilst the fence posts and buildings are favoured by Whinchats.

Stand just about anywhere to witness pipits, larks, Swallows and martins passing through, and look up for migrating Honey Buzzards - a regular late spring and September feature, whilst Black Kites have been recorded here more than anywhere else on the island.

Coombe Bottom is the place to go in summer to enjoy some of the best chalk grassland in Europe, full of Pyramidal and Burnt-tip Orchids. Adonis Blue butterflies and Dark Green Fritillaries are present in good numbers.

Steephill and Rew Down

THIS SMALL AREA OF fine quality, south facing chalk downland has proven to be one of the best spots for grounded migrants and observing visible migration.

Walk west along Steephill Down Road. The line of scrub and Sycamores to your right, as you walk west along the first section of road, is a real sun trap and, during September and October, is often alive with Phyloscs, and smaller numbers of Blackcaps, Whitethroats and Spotted Flycatchers.

Continue along Steephill Down Road. Up off to your right, there's a public footpath heading up between the cemetery edge and an abandoned, scrubby quarry. This small area is a magnet for Whinchats, Phyloscs, Sylvia warblers, Redstarts and flycatchers. This area often holds migrants throughout the day - indeed, it often appears to fill up with birds as the day progresses and the sun warms the south-west facing scrub.

As you enter the Local Nature Reserve, check the fence line down to the south - this is a great spot for flycatchers and chats. The open chalk grassland and golf course on the summit of the downs is good for Wheatears.

Week and Dean Farms

ON THE EAST SIDE OF St Lawrence Shute, just as it dips down through the inner cliff face into the 'lowlands' of St Lawrence itself, is a small, triangular arable field owned by the Hampshire & Isle of Wight Wildlife Trust. It is managed as a traditional cereal field for its arable flora, and has proven itself to be truly fantastic for buntings and finches. Rarely watched, surely some real jems must find this field but remain undetected - rare buntings, pipits and larks?

Over St Lawrence Shute, walk west along the inner cliff top to view arable and grassy fields inland, and the Undercliff below. The clifftop scrub attracts the occasional Ring Ouzels and is excellent for Redstarts; check the arable for Wheatears and who knows what else!

High Hat and Niton Radar Station

BETWEEN NITON IN THE west and St Lawrence Shute in the east, the inner cliff is backed by expansive arable fields with little cover.

This forms an abrupt transition between the well-wooded Undercliff below to the south, and very exposed, open farmland stretching off inland.

This area is excellent for concentrating migrants, especially in spring.

The inner cliff-top shrubs form a linear habitat, the inland (north-west) face of which is where the migrants concentrate. These are very easy to see as they feed along the shrubby edge along which the clifftop public right-of-way runs. In spring, late in the day, the sun illuminates the face of this shrub line. Migrants move inland from within the Undercliff and feed enthusiastically here.

Away from Ventnor Downs, I've found this to be the most reliable area to count grounded migrants. In view of its position and the commanding views it affords both of the Undercliff below and inland, this is likely an excellent visible migration vantage point. But I've yet to test this.

The clifftop walk extends around 4km east to west, and one can easily walk to or from St Catherine's Point along this walk.

The Radar Station is a rather dilapidated fenced enclosure with a small building, radar towers and wires. It is encircled by wooden and wire fences and patches of shrubs. Redstarts and Spotted Flycatchers favour this area.

To the west of the Radar Station the huge, open arable fields extend for several kilometres along the cliff top and a kilometre or so inland. These fields are often cropped with spring cereals owing to their wild, windswept exposure. They can be excellent for larks and pipits in autumn, with these, and Yellowhammers and Linnets a fixture in winter.

Who knows what else one might find. One mustn't enter this private land, but rather scan across it. But there is a public footpath across it between the cliff top and the nearby village of Niton. This affords excellent mid-field views.

None of this area is visited with any regularity by birders and it alone would reward concerted coverage.

Further inland: Nettlecombe and Wydcombe

I'LL ONLY BRIEFLY OUTLINE the birding potential of the farmland inland from the Undercliff. It's for you to discover and report back!

The National Trust farmland at Wydcombe hosted nesting Bee Eaters a few years ago. Largely grassland with numerous wet flushes and streams, this area is little visited by anyone, let alone birders, but is essentially open access and would constitute an interesting local patch.

The privately-owned Downcourt Farm had some excellent arable until around 2018 when it was unfortunately reverted to species-poor grassland.

Further east, the grassland around the Nettlecombe Fish Ponds is largely tightly grazed by sheep and rarely watched. The ponds themselves are open and more than likely attract the odd interesting duck. There's rarely any muddy edges to speak of unfortunately.

5. Other Isle of Wight bird watching sites

I very rarely leave the Undercliff! So I can't really give an authoritative account of where else to go birding on the Isle of Wight.

I will attempt to give a incomplete overview of some key areas though.

St Catherines Point

The westernmost tip of the Undercliff and southernmost point on the island, St Catherines Point (SCP) provides the best sea watching opportunity and much the same land bird migration experience as the rest of the Undercliff. The area is very under watched and would benefit from more concerted coverage. One can park in the Windy Corner car park and gain access to much of the best habitat.

Solent coast and estuaries

The waterfowl and shorebird enthusiast will certainly want to visit the Solent coast and associated small harbours and estuaries.

The central chalk ridge

Extending between The Needles in the west and Culver Cliff in the east, a ridge of chalk extends across the centre of the island. On the south slope of this ridge, areas of species-rich chalk grassland and chalk shrublands are excellent for landbird migrants. There are scattered Ash woodlands on the more shady north slopes and within vales and coombes.

The Needles and West High Down

The tall, west protruding promontory of the Needles represents an obvious landfall for migrating birds. There is limited cover towards the western end of the promontory, increasing the chance that one might unearth something scarce. To my eye, this whole area probably represents the greatest potential to find rare landbirds on the island. Rarities have included Alpine Accentor and Hume's Warbler.

Brook and Mottistone downs

The chalk ridge continues east from West High Down broken only by the mouth of the Western Yar at Freshwater Bay. Visiting birders found a fine singing male Black-headed Bunting on the south facing chalk at Compton Down one May recently. A local bird found a Melodious Warbler on the coastal clifftop at Sudmoor in April 2023.

Culver Cliff

The very eastern end of the central chalk ridge terminates at Culver Cliff. This rather shrubby area of chalk downland is owned by the National Trust. It's an obvious spot to look for landbird migrants. The hilltop also provides an excellent vantage point from which to view down across the RSPB Brading Marshes reserve below. Both Little Swift and Woodchat Shrike have been seen at Foreland Fields just below Culver and to the north-east.

Woodlands

The island supports numerous small woodlands and several large pine-dominated forestry plantations. Oaks dominate natural woodlands north of the central chalk, with Ash dominated woodlands in the south of the island. Several plantation forests support Nightjar. Nightingale is present in several wetter woodlands in the north of the island.

Freshwater wetlands

The RSPB nature reserve at Brading Marshes represents the premier freshwater wetland on the island. Typical species include Bittern, passage waders and wintering waterfowl.

Farmland

Much of the island is farmed. This farmland is fairly typical in terms of the birds to be found. Yellowhammers are reasonably common particularly in the south of the island. The tiny population of Corn Bunting once present along the Military Road is sadly now extinct

Military Road valleys

The flat coastal plain along the Military Road is comprised a mix of large, exposed arable farmland in the east, around Chale (once supporting a small Corn Bunting population) and more intricate field systems further west around Mottistone. The small, deeply-incised coastal valleys (Chines) where streams cascade into the sea can be good for concentrating migrants, though they're often not as productive as one might expect. Migrants appear to favour the higher ground of the chalk downs in the south of the island and The Needles and Culver Cliff. That said, the exposed arable farmland itself, and any isolated patches of cover embedded within it, might reward more attention.

6. Bird Observatory Project

Situated roughly midway along the south coast, with the Portland Bird Observatory off to the west, and Dungeness Bird Observatory off to the east, the Isle of Wight is perhaps an obvious gap in the UK Bird Observatory network.

The need for a Bird Observatory on the island has been pondered by the author of this book for some time. In 2023, steps are afoot to look at the feasibility of establishing one.

This section provides a short account of the concept. Feasibility study work is ongoing.

As documented elsewhere in this book, the island is superb for observing bird migration. It is also rich in wider biodiversity. A Bird Observatory here, conducting intensive biodiversity monitoring and conservation work, could have a significant impact.

Activities of an Isle of Wight Bird Observatory

Below we identify a few early activities a charity - a Bird Observatory Trust, affiliated with the UK Bird Observatory Council - might engage in.

<u>Constant effort recording</u>: the core activity of the Bird Observatory would, of course, be to establish and maintain thorough monitoring of bird and wildlife communities within its project area. This would include constant effort ringing, daily rounds of recording areas, and timed seabird counts.

Land acquisition: the Bird Observatory would include a land trust component. It would seek to acquire, through freehold purchase or leasing, plots of land to be managed optimally for wildlife. This would aim to replicate the experience at the Portland Bird Observatory, where land acquisition is now a core and highly effective, if somewhat capital intensive, function. Like Portland, we'd likely acquire relatively small plots initially. These would be managed to provide arable type habitats, because very high quality wintering habitat for seed-eating birds is seen as a key problem facing birds of conservation concern. We would also look to acquire wetlands or areas with the potential to create wetlands. Acquisition would focus within the Undercliff and on the farmland immediately inland of it in the early years.

Islandwide conservation projects: the Bird Observatory would look to set up a breeding birds survey style programme across the island. This might aim to increase the number of 1km squares surveyed by island birders to enable the development of an Isle of Wight specific bird index and population monitoring scheme. It would also aim to advocate for bird and wildlife conservation and support the work of existing organisations such the the Hampshire & Isle of Wight Wildlife Trust and RSPB.

Delivering farm advice: much of the Isle of Wight is farmland. There is enormous potential to greatly enhance the wildlife value of our farmland without compromising food production. The Observatory would therefore work with island farmers to find opportunities to enhance the quality of farmland for wildlife.

Showing people birds and wildlife: a core activity for the Bird Observatory would be to celebrate the island's wildlife and to show it to people in a way that avoids any disturbance.

Supporting scientific research: the Bird Observatory would aim to establish partnerships with universities in order to support research on the island by students. Possible research projects could focus on Red Squirrels, White-tailed Sea Eagles, Dormice, Glanville Fritillary butterflies, and the broad range of specialist bees and wasps found within the Undercliff.

International twinning and conservation programme:

The Bird Observatory Trust would look to twin with nature reserve creation organisations in the tropics. Twinning would enable it to start to raise funds to support tropical nature reserve expansion and management. One possible fundraising theme would be to support the acquisition of a tropical nature reserve in, say, Colombia or Ecuador, of a similar size to the Isle of Wight.

Initial components of a Bird Observatory

The very first step to establishing a Bird Observatory would be to define the overall project area, and recording areas within it.

The current proposal is to establish an initial base for the Bird Observatory within the Undercliff on the island's south east facing coastline - the area covered by this booklet.

Although St Catherines Point would be the obvious place to establish this base, opportunities there seem rather limited.

We are therefore looking for further east within St Lawrence. Centrally positioned within the Undercliff, such a base would provide easier access to prime migration spots such as Ventnor Downs and St Lawrence itself, as well as St Catherines Point.

We will establish a small group to take the feasibility work forward. If this looks promising, we will look to formally establish a charity regulated by the The Charity Commission.

We would devise a business plan, fundraising plan, and secure initial funding to employ a seasonal Observatory manager.

The initial Bird Observatory base would likely comprise a simple space similar to that at the Holme Bird Observatory in Norfolk. This would provide a welcoming point of contact for island birders and naturalists and visitors.

The Bird Observatory manager would be responsible for leading further fundraising, promotion, local liaison, and the recruitment of teams of volunteers to support various projects.

Accommodation?

At the time of writing it is proposed not to provide accommodation for visitors in the first instance. Rather, we would establish partnerships with existing accommodation providers. These are numerous and varied within the Undercliff. We would encourage visitors to use high quality recommended accommodation.

Supporting the project

Soon, we will create a project website. This will include a donations tab. Should a Bird Observatory prove not to be feasible, funds will be re-directed to a tropical nature reserve land acquisition project. Keep searching for 'Isle of Wight Bird Observatory' on Google. The website will likely appear in due course. The project can be contacted by leaving a comment on its YouTube channel: https://www.youtube.com/channel/UCWg3ZLyIB24DbvQ-Wrr98Lg

7. Acknowledgements

Thanks to Blakes Tea Hut, Toni's Tea Room, Lady Scarlett's and Besty & Spinky on Ventnor beach for keeping me supplied with coffee, tea, and toast and marmite. Thanks to Nick Lever for providing the sea watching text. Thanks to the Ventnor community for being nice.

8. About the author

Steve Jones worked in UK and International conservation for a couple of decades before becoming a researcher and some-time biogeography lecturer. He now focuses on writing and is establishing a charity focused on supporting the tropical nature reserve creation efforts of communities in the Andes and Southeast Asia. Find out more at stevecjones.uk[1]

Accompanying maps

YOU'LL FIND A ROUGH map of the area on the following page. I've created some site videos that complement the text here. I'll add a map to the channel soon. These can be viewed in video form at the *Isle of Wight Bird Observatory* YouTube channel here: https://www.youtube.com/playlist?list=PLXsfprjfB6v38q136mWyTVerKFtKwVj39

And at my own YouTube channel, *Steve Jones Wild Writer*, here: https://www.youtube.com/channel/UCWg3ZLyIB24DbvQ-Wrr98Lg

---

1. http://stevecjones.uk

Printed in Great Britain
by Amazon